Values have power.

Use them well.

How to harness your values to
create a high-performance culture.

Erika Clegg
The voice for values

Produced by Softwood Books, Suffolk, UK

First Edition

Paperback ISBN: 978-1-3999-7387-8

www.swspublishing.com

www.larkenby.com

CONTENTS

INTRODUCTION

March 23rd, 2020: for the first time ever, under greater curbs even than at the height of the London Blitz, Britain was placed into Lockdown.

Events, parties and schools stopped. Appointments, meetings and office working stopped. Travel, exercise and commuting stopped. Business stopped.

The phrase of the time became "Now, more than ever..." and then, more than ever, culture mattered. Businesses with a thriving values-driven culture found it hard but could weather the sudden ripping apart of their teams to work from kitchen tables, box rooms, children's bedrooms and garden sheds; even to be furloughed for an uncertain period of time.

The early rollercoaster of the Pandemic gave company directors a sudden opportunity to flex their leadership muscles and make tough choices. Some found it nigh on impossible without the scaffold of embedded values to bounce off and lean on. Teams with common purpose and shared vision had stronger glue than those without. The loss of watercooler moments and serendipitous idea generation had to be replaced - open and ongoing communication was the only way.

Of course some excellent companies were unlucky, too: but of those who could maintain their offer or pivot to meet changed needs, a strong company culture was essential to survive and thrive.

This book shares some stories of businesses, organisations, and even a country, that have grown their place in the world by defining their values and living by them.

Organisations with a high-functioning culture rise head and shoulders above their competitors when it comes to talent attraction, development and retention; brand profile, loyalty and value; investor attraction, and commercial performance.

How is that level of culture formed?

When values permeate every aspect of organisations' work, and are understood and lived by everyone, they become culture. Without clear values, or the actions around them, it's likely that culture will be formed in other ways and not by the business leaders.

But the challenge many of those business leaders face is how to bring their values to life fully. Too often they become little more than a box ticked, and have meagre impact on behaviour and outcomes. What can be done to improve that?

Larkenby's positioning line is:

Every company has values.
Very few have Active Ethos.

And in that simple phrase lies the answer. Over the next pages you'll find that answer, and many others.

You'll read stories of extraordinary transformations driven by values and culture.

You'll look into your own values, finding some tools that will cause you to challenge and maybe change them.

And you'll start to create a plan for your own business's culture change.

I can assure you of a high energy and goal-driven experience which will leave you excited for the future and focused on a plan to help you get there.

In this book you will:

Discover Active Ethos	**Test your personal values**
Learn why it matters	**Find out how to create great corporate values**
Read some stories of culture	**Start an Active Ethos plan**

SECTION 1

THEORY

Chapter 1
Why am I writing this book?

In 2006, my husband and I left our London careers to launch a creative communications agency in the pretty seaside town of Southwold, Suffolk. It was a leap of faith but over the 17 years we owned it we built it up into a great business.

We positioned ourselves as The Agency for Change, and as a result of that we were working with people in client businesses who had a real appetite for brave steps and transformative choices. It was exciting and fulfilling work, and I could see my ambitions to make an impact starting to bear fruit in this brave business with its growing profile.

Clients near and far benefited from the agency's moon-shot approach, and so over the years we won diverse projects including Moroccan national tourism, community consultation for the Sizewell C project, a water resilience fairground for Anglian Water, and launching Champagne Bollinger's digital presence.

Look back to 2015 and all the external signs were great: headcount up, turnover up, new clients up. But - as you'd expect from this book's existence - things were not up, up, up. The malaise was clear from our client retention rates, which were falling; and that was impacting our reputation and profitability.

When you own a business its reputation is your reputation, its profit directly impacts not only its survival but also your income, so something had to be done.

At the base of the problem was my own cowardice. I should have been having tough conversations about service levels, but I didn't have the skills to start them. And so things were likely to get worse.

As fate would have it, someone I knew vaguely - largely through his reputation as a high profile business leader - had decided to become a business coach with Vistage, and was looking for members to join his first group.

His name is David Sheepshanks and his first email to me included the unlocking line: "It can be lonely at the top of an organisation.".

Vistage is American in origin, and gives its members three advantages: direct coaching by an experienced Chair, peer but non-competitive CEO group members, and access to world-class specialist business speakers.

Vistage's approach of looking at people in the round - helping them across all areas of their lives, not just business - appealed to me, juggling challenges at work but also with child care, parents and other aspects of life outside the office. So I joined, becoming his first member.

The second speaker we had was Pete Wilkinson, whose one-page business plan appealed to me as someone who likes to cut things right down to the most simple version that will still work. I took it back to the business, not just for a company plan but also to form the basis of monthly one-to-one sessions for every member of the team.

We weren't quite having the difficult conversations yet, but spending time on each team member's ambitions and challenges started to create a positive sense across the business, and a marked increase in ambition and combined productivity.

The 'sliding door' moment, however, was in a Floyd Woodrow workshop.

The background to this was my growing sense that I needed to clarify my values. It seemed to me that many of the issues in my business were down to the fact that our corporate values were in place but as far as I could tell they had no impact on anyone's choices or behaviours.

Added to that, we had reached a scale where my lived values, which had underlined our culture, would no longer be picked up intuitively by the whole team. I was keen to define them in words and at the back of my mind I was vaguely forming an idea of using them for the business too.

Floyd came to talk to us about his North Star and compass concept, and in endeavouring to clarify my purpose - another matter that had been troubling me - I suddenly found my values drop, half formed, from the ether.

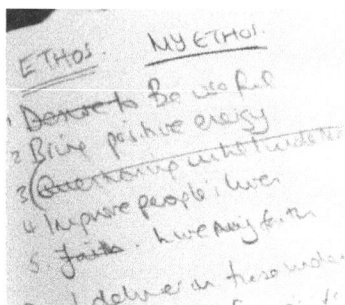

To cut a long story short, it was from these that, with the team, we drew up the agency values which were as follows:

1. Bring Positive Energy

2. Know What Matters

3. Make Excellent Work

4. Improve People's Lives

5. Live our Vision (as Agents for Change.)

Over the course of the next four years, without realising it, I spearheaded my first Active Ethos programme by ensuring the values underpinned every action and decision taken in that business.

The change was palpable, as we peeled back layers of cultural assumption and started again from the core, building it entirely round our new values set. Clients were given the values as the heart of a guarantee, partners and suppliers signed SLAs built on them, people were recruited, mentored and rewarded through them.

All that and much more besides drove us towards a values-driven culture, with me front and centre, pushing, pulling and keeping it all powering towards success.

Over the course of the first two years our team halved in size as people who did not feel connected to the new approach stepped away. It was a painful period for all concerned but a necessary one to build from. And what emerged was a united, ambitious team with shared aims, the ability to have robust conversations (since the values gave everyone the tools for candour, not just me), and a clear sense of connection to the agency's values and culture.

This was demonstrated by our results.

Counterintuitively, whilst our headcount plummeted, our inbound calls and turnover continued to rise: as did retention, reputation and profit. Together we had flipped all the arrows back into the right direction, creating a healthy, sustainable business with an exceptional team which could now grow from firm foundations.

I now found myself with another problem, one that any company owner would be only too pleased to have. With a team whose members had grown in skills and ambition at an exponential rate, where was there for them to go?

I realised that I was standing in the way of their continued advancement. You might say there was an Erika Ceiling.

Luckily, this coincided with me having two discoveries - one, after two decades I had taken my agency career as far as I wanted it to go, and two, I had become completely obsessed with the benefit that values and culture brought to business, when done right.

And so, in early 2022, after an 18 month programme of change, the senior leadership team took over the business through MBO and I stepped out of the career that had been my passion since my early teens, and into a total focus on values and culture.

It's energising and exciting and a real privilege to share with other people through workshops, commissions and this book. Funnily enough I don't worry about my purpose anymore: I have found it.

Chapter 2
But first, this ...

Please do not resort to Google, your company website or asking a colleague. Can you write down your corporate values from memory? I have provided eight spaces though it's unlikely you will need this many.

1.

2.

3.

4.

5.

6.

7.

8.

Now, can you consider and jot down how these values - individually and as a complete set - are used to improve your organisation's performance?

And finally, give your team a mark out of ten for embodying your values:

/ 10

As you work through the rest of this book, you'll want to come back to what you've written here, so stick a bookmark in or fold the page to keep it handy.

Chapter 3
What is Active Ethos?

For a start, let's look at what values are. One of the best explanations I've ever come across can be found in the Army Leadership Code.

> *Values are specific beliefs that people have about what is important and unimportant, good and bad, right and wrong.*
>
> *Values develop out of our direct experiences with people who are important to us and have impact on our lives.*
>
> *When values are declared and followed, they form the basis of trust. When they are not stated, they are often inferred from observable behaviour. When they are stated and not followed, trust is broken.*

It's worth unpicking that third paragraph.

The ideal situation is given in the first sentence: 'When values are declared and followed, they form the basis of trust.'.

In other words, say what you do and do what you say.

It doesn't matter what your values are, whether people like them or not: if you state them clearly and your behaviour reflects them, people know what they are getting and can therefore trust you.

The second sentence, 'When they are not stated, they are often inferred from observable behaviour.' echoes the famous saying that 'culture is what happens when you're not in the room'. I liken it to the kids on the back seat of the school bus: if there are not clear values in place, the rebels will set the tone.

It's rare in this day and age to have a company that doesn't state its values, but it's what they do with them leads us onto the third and most pertinent statement: 'When they are stated and not followed, trust is broken.'. This gives a clue to the meaning of Active Ethos.

It's quite clear that if you say one thing and do another, people will not know what to expect.

That means they lose trust.

What is less obvious is that this applies to everyone in your organisation, and every action taken.

It's easy to forget the people at the front line of customer relations - the part-time bartender, the lunchtime receptionist - but for many of your clients, they are the first and only point of connection with your business. Their approach gives those clients their sole insight to your culture.

So it's essential that the values you state are evident in everyone's behaviour. (And yes, that includes yours.)

I firmly believe in stretch values. Values set a standard that people have to push to reach. So on that basis, we have to ask the question "Why?".

Why would everyone want to make an effort? I am very often told early on in a project that people in one part of the business are never going to buy into this because they are not passionate about their work, and never will be.

To that, I call piffle.

People need a reason to make an effort. We all feel better with something ahead of us that's worth aiming for. And so you need to bring another element into your work: a vision.

Here, I refer to that titan of philosophy: Winnie the Pooh. Says AA Milne in the very first story he wrote about the 100 Acre Wood's inhabitants:

"He could see the honey, he could smell the honey, but he couldn't quite reach the honey."

What matters most to Winnie the Pooh? Why is it worth a 'tubby old bear' making the effort?

Winnie the Pooh loves honey. To see it, smell it, have it tantalisingly just out of reach is motivation enough to encourage him to really push himself.

(Those who know the story will know this was a moon shot, and ultimately he failed - but not without huge effort that delivered its own rewards.)

This is why it's so important to craft your vision in a way that appeals to your people.

As a board you will have copious numerical metrics - dates, currency, percentage points and more. The purpose of these combined is to create something progressive.

You probably find it exciting and inspiring in its raw state: but it's unlikely that numbers and KPIs will ping everyone's elastic in the same way. If you can package your signs and symbols of progress up in an exciting way then you have a vision that motivates everyone.

What is their North Star, their 100 metres gold, their moon landing, their honey?

Find the symbols of achievement, couch it in the language they use, and stitch it into your communications, internally and externally.

And so we come to Active Ethos.

This diagram shows how vision and values form a powerful alliance to drive purposeful behaviour. It's this combination that forms Active Ethos: the relentless application of a really well-expressed values set, with everyone united towards a common goal, that delivers exceptional company culture.

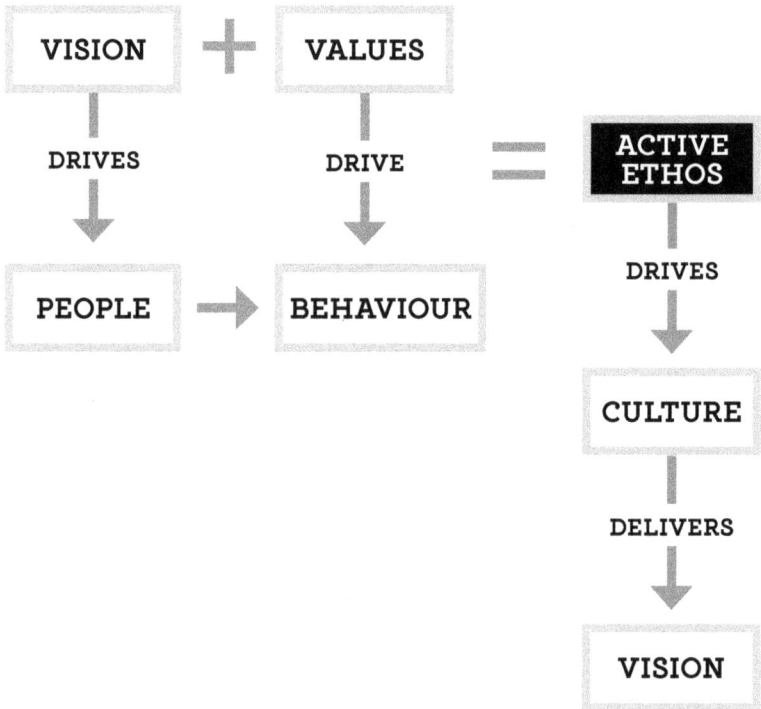

VISION + VALUES

VISION DRIVES → PEOPLE → BEHAVIOUR

VALUES DRIVE → BEHAVIOUR

= ACTIVE ETHOS

ACTIVE ETHOS DRIVES → CULTURE

CULTURE DELIVERS → VISION

A vision that's defined to appeal to your people's motivations will inspire them to behave in a way that's driven by your values. It's this reaction to the vision that means you can build in stretch values.

So your vision really has to work for a living!

The process of vision and values working together is called Active Ethos, and it's that which drives an excellent culture that will then deliver the vision which has inspired your people. It becomes a virtuous circle.

Michelle Obama says:

"There is no magic to achievement. It's really about hard work, choices and persistence."

That sums up very well that virtuous circle of vision, compelling people to behave in a way that's driven by values.

This sustained process is the 'active' part of Active Ethos, and it's that which allows your stated values to be followed, creating trust.

We can push this one step further, with another 'why?'.

I often encounter a prevailing mood of cynicism from a company's wider team upon first starting a project with them. That's only to be expected - if everyone in an organisation was an advocate of values-led culture, I wouldn't need to be there.

Throughout the course of a project the benefits of the process reveal themselves. And so people move from going through the motions with some reluctance, to advocacy.

However, at the starting point of this exercise it's respectful to explain why culture matters.

After all, if the vision is your people's 'why', then achieving a strong culture to get you all there is yours.

IBM's former chief executive, Louis Gerstner, says

"I came to see in my time at IBM, that culture isn't just one aspect of the game - it is the game. In the end, an organization is nothing more than the collective capacity of its people to create value."

With the phrase 'no-one ever got fired for hiring IBM' ringing in our ears, this view is powerful. And it's backed up by data.

According to Gallup, companies with good culture are 21% more profitable and see 41% less absenteeism.

An 11-year programme using 263 research studies across 192 organisations in 49 industries and 34 countries demonstrated a difference of over 500% revenue growth between organisations with a thriving company culture and without.

47% of people actively seeking a new job cited corporate culture as their reason for leaving, 37% prized recognition above all else, and only 29% were happy with their development. Consider the cost and risks of replacing staff and the impact starts to loom.

And what of your clients and customers?

These days, brand image cannot be controlled by its owners - the outside world knows too much, sees too much to allow this. Authenticity is not a buzzword, it's essential to brand growth and people are looking for organisations with purpose to discover and share.

Culture, communicated makes the difference.

Look at the success of Patagonia, whose values mirror those of its target market: it grew 30% in one year alone, the year when its Christmas ad said "Don't buy this jacket".

Culture drives engagement and reputation, and Active Ethos is the way to bring it wholeheartedly into your organisation through a tightly managed, well documented and highly collaborative process.

Let's consider some of the benefits of Active Ethos in our own organisations.

Start by scribbling your starting thoughts on what these might be, and the areas of your business it could influence. This should take you about ten minutes.

When you've done, turn the page to discover more. You can go back to your list and add any more that resonate when you've read through them.

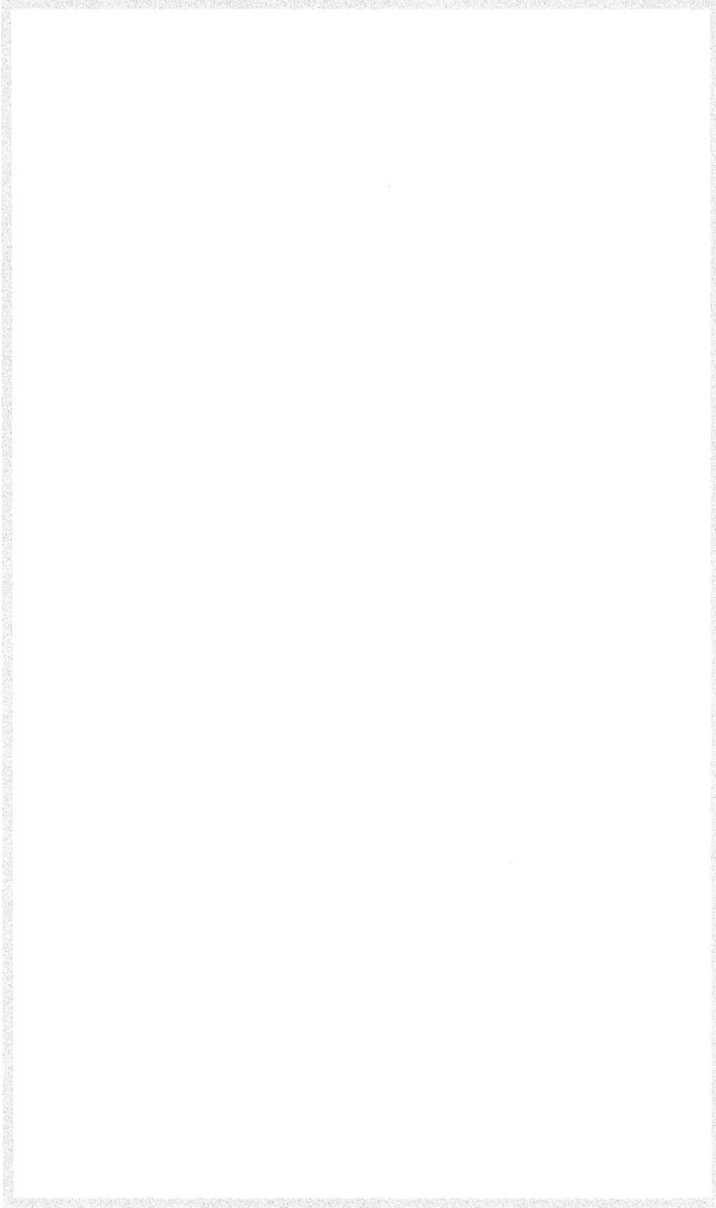

Here are just some places you'll find Active Ethos

TEAM

- Development
- Recruitment
- Retention
- Morale
- Loyalty
- Responsibility

QUALITY CONTROL

- Personal accountability
- Peer accountability
- Standard setting
- Pride

SALES

- Clarity
- Messaging
- Guarantee expectations
- Visibility
- Contracts

BRAND

- Desirability
- Standout
- Value
- Authenticity
- Reputation

PERFORMANCE

- Efficiency
- Profitability
- Striving
- Growth

INDUSTRY PEERS

- Exemplar status
- Recognition
- Talent magnet
- M&A benefits

By this stage, you will be starting to form some useful thoughts on ways to bring your values more fully to life to benefit your organisation and its people.

In that context I'd like to ask you to focus back for a minute, with this new insight, and have a cold hard glance at where you feel the organisational culture sits now.

Where is your bar? And where would you like it to be?

Think of that goal as a mini-vision to drive this process and help you maintain your vigour as you take it forward.

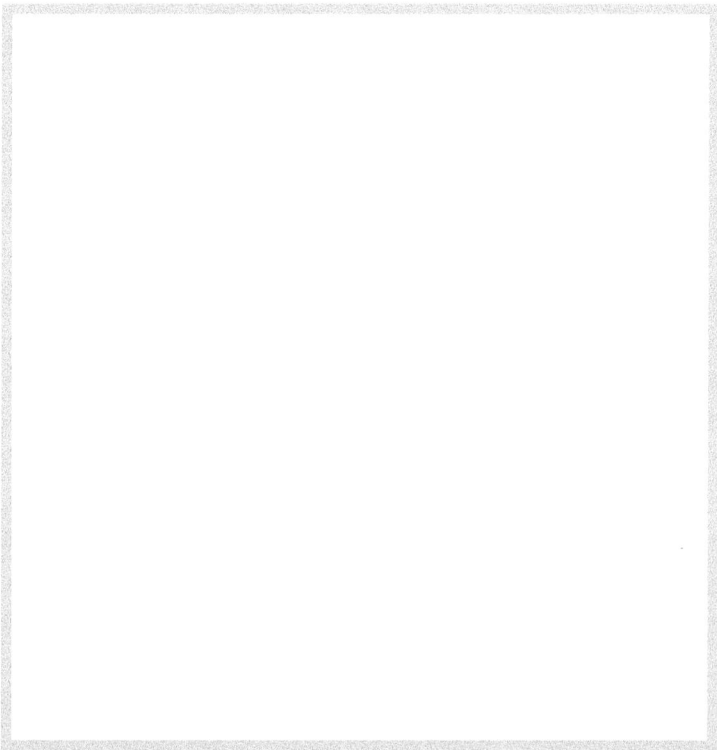

We'll round off with some quick thoughts about what Active Ethos does and doesn't do, as a useful crib sheet.

Active Ethos does:

Set the bar high

Allow you to change things

Wrap round all processes

Define shape of talent management

Underpin your marketing

Set expectations in partner relationships

Give you competitive advantage

Need constant maintenance.

Active Ethos doesn't:

Have to be 'nice'

... and nor do you

Confine itself to one department

Cause unnecessary work

Cost anything

Count, if you ignore it

Look after itself.

Chapter 4
Stories of Culture

HMP LIVERPOOL

'Squalid' was the word used to describe HMP Liverpool in 2017. Rioting prisoners and striking staff from this men's prison were making their feelings clear about the semi-derelict environment, with smashed windows, peeling paint and uncared for outside spaces. Drugs were rife, even flown in on drones through the broken windows.

The prison inspectorate described the problem as a 'failure of leadership on all levels' and helicoptered in Pia Sinha: a psychologist, diminutive in stature and big on guts and vision.

Pia set about transforming the prison, drawing in the prison staff, inmates and community from the off. At the heart of their work was a clever set of values:

1. **Rebuilding trust**
2. **Creating hope**
3. **Believing in the future**

What's really smart about them, and something to which all values should aspire, is their ability to attach themselves to everybody involved, and a wide range of situations.

There was an immediate crisis which had seen trust eroded, lack of hope and no future focus - to turn it around would require all three to be remedied. But stepping aside from that, the core of the prison offer has the same requirement for its inmates: and, one might argue, often for them with the world. Pia built progress around a set of sustainable, truthful values which at the time must have felt like a big stretch.

Over the course of eighteen months everybody pulled together, with the prisoners themselves playing a major role in the improvements. From the skills required for woodwork, building, plastering, painting and window repairs, to a successful submission for £4m to get an astroturf football field which also hosted the first prison Park Run, inmates were learning transferable skills even as they improved their environment.

Pia firmly believed in the power of participation, and praised all three of her stakeholder groups - prisoners, staff and community members - for having got 'stuck in' when, at the end of the programme of improvements, the same prison inspector lavished praise on them for 'a culture of care' with a 'real change in the quality of leadership'. The turnaround was complete.

THE JOY CLUB

On the 14th March 2021, LSE graduate and keen sailor Hannah Thomson secured funding to launch a business inspired by her granny. It was part of the growing move towards online experience, and it would prove both timely and spectacularly challengingly timed in one.

A few weeks later Britain was in Lockdown: a greater curb on movement than even that seen in the World Wars of the early 20th century. This of course made Hannah's idea - a website offering live classes to members up and down the British Isles - land at exactly the right time for an elderly audience that suddenly found itself completely isolated, even more so than before in a society where elderly isolation was a growing epidemic.

Where the challenge lay, however, was in Hannah's leadership of her team. Her experience of leadership came from sailing, where you are never more than a metre away from your colleagues. Suddenly Hannah found herself with a new business bringing a new concept to market through a new team: all of them working virtually.

Driven by her clear vision for the business, Hannah first created a set of values for the business, to get it off the ground, but when the team reached 12 people she invited them to work together on a set that would see The Joy Club into its next stages, leading the process themselves. Sharing stories of their passions and frustrations led to a two-part framework of values and stretch factors. Values would be shared everywhere, and set out beliefs and unifying issues; stretch factors would be internal measures against which team members judged themselves and each other.

VALUES:

1. Celebration
2. Collaboration
3. Making a difference

STRETCH FACTORS:

1. Experimental
2. Adaptable
3. Getting sh*t done

All of these items were tested and forged in the heat of a global pandemic. And as ever, they gave Hannah and her team the resources they needed to make tough decisions, to pivot, to turn the standard model on its head from the start and emerge from it stronger.

All the rules of values application to create culture were followed: the whole team bonded to make sure efforts are observed and rewarded, to bounce ideas off one another and to get to know each other well. Daily Zoom meetings, real world events including a Chelsea Flower Show garden, celebration bells on Slack, campaigning with members on their issues - and as the world adapted the infrastructure became more accessible around them.

The next funding waves were managed entirely online, partnerships forged with retirement villages, corporates and charities, the team grew to encompass people by talent not geography, and within two years The Joy Club had over 10,000 members, hundreds of success stories, and had secured millions of pounds of funding to keep developing the platform for its fans.

Members reported feeling fully part of something, and 94% said they felt less lonely. "It is a gentle and welcoming place to be and be part of" said one: a great achievement for a demographic more likely to socialise and learn in real life.

BREWDOG

What's fascinating about BrewDog - who, as we all know, are lovable scamps - is that four of their five values entirely justify their more outlandish behaviour. Had they left it at four they could reasonably argue that people knew exactly what to expect of them and didn't have a leg to stand on in trying to complain.

Because values don't have to be nice. Values are not about imposing the world's views on you, but are about stating your world view. It's a very different thing and I'd say that BrewDog's values set is 80% exemplary.

BREWDOG'S VALUES

1. We bleed craft beer
2. We are uncompromising
3. We are geeks
4. We blow shit up

Let's deconstruct that. It's quite blokey. The 'we' makes it clear that everyone is expected to buy into it. Whilst one of them is very specific - bleed craft beer - the others are open to a range of situations, if not interpretations. Uncompromising makes its point very clear indeed, whatever your point of connection. And if you were expecting an organisation to observe etiquette, 'blow shit up' would shatter the illusion.

But hold on, you say: that's only four. You said they have five.

Indeed they do: and this is it.

5. Without us, we are nothing.

Now, I don't know about you, but that looks like it belongs to a completely different company. My instinct is that it was added as a compromise. In fact, since discovering this I have observed that many sets of corporate values have a team-related item last, which is ironic, when you think about it.

It's on account of that value that 'Punks with Purpose' - a renegade band of ex-employees and anonymous existing staff - could reasonably and justifiably create a massive social media problem for James Watt to pick his way through, clearly in unfamiliar territory.

When I describe BrewDog's values as pretty much exemplary I can feel the air being sucked out of the room by the sudden, sharp intakes of breath around me. I know how a vacuum-packed sausage feels. But it's true: values are your values, not those other people would like you to have, or would choose for themselves. And in that regard, BrewDog's are (80%) brilliant.

COSATTO

If you've bought baby care equipment in the last decade or so, and want to avoid the sea of beige or gender-specific colours, you might well have gravitated towards Cosatto: 'baby stuff with personality'.

Launched in the early 80's, Cosatto was at first an old fashioned 'baby stuff' business with the call-a-spade-a-shovel name of Pram Corner. The ambition was there from the start, and over the next few decades it grew, partially through acquisitions, renamed itself and steered towards its USP. One thing it lost, however, was its sense of fun and family, and when the 2008 recession hit, Cosatto hit the rocks and went into partial administration owing £4m to the bank.

How would you find your way back from that?

Here's how Andrew Kluge, who shared his story with me, did it. He was completely honest. He said to the team "We've got a mountain to climb, but there is a chance if we all pull together. There are no guarantees. Some of the things we are doing are risky but it is the only way.".

In truth survival was very unlikely. They restructured, and of the original team of 75, 35 stayed taking a 10% pay cut in exchange for a bonus scheme that was built round complete financial transparency. Nobody expected the profits, incidentally, and initially much of the financial information was way out of comfort zones for some: but every month, good and bad was shared and training given to explain things. Amazingly, Cosatto started to pull through.

In year one, everyone received an 11% bonus.

It had been about survival and paying off the bank. By 2011 most of the loan was paid back, and the team could recalibrate. Andrew believes that the CEO's number one job is values and culture, and he understands that it's a marathon not a sprint.

To ensure open mindedness, he brought in consultants to lead the process. It took 18 months to develop, test and update their values set - or, in their words, 'How we do stuff at Cosatto, and why we do it'. That led them to 12 statements, and a year later a 13th was added.

1. **Just do it**
2. **Stand up and be counted**
3. **Finish what we start**
4. **Do the right thing**
5. **Show respect, give support and, above all, care**
6. **Dot the i's and cross the t's**
7. **Look after the pennies**
8. **Say what you mean and mean what you say**
9. **Fly the flag**
10. **Go the extra mile**
11. **Enjoy the ride and get happy**
12. **Keep raising the bar**
13. **Think outside the box**

There might be a lot of them, but Cosatto does a lot to keep them circulating and ensure each of the values does its job for the business. They're also clear: nice active statements, in familiar language that makes them stick in the mind and trip off the tongue.

Monthly awards celebrate the values, the 'C-Factor' allows people to score their colleagues against them, tinypulse technology sits behind 'cheers for peers' and people receive handwritten letters to congratulate them on meeting a value. There is so much trust in the culture that Cosatto has fully adopted 3R's working (Results, Responsibility, Relaxation) so there are no set hours or holidays, with every member of the team making their own choices about how to deliver on their role.

And then came 2020, and a global pandemic - another huge challenge for the business. "Without a massively strong culture I don't think we would have survived." says Andrew. The 3R's principle had set them up for working from home, and everyone intuitively checked in on their colleagues. Serendipity was simulated via Zoom, and directors ensured regular contact with everyone. Attention switched from B2B2C which had been the model - selling to retailers, to sell to consumers - to direct consumer sales online, which has grown exponentially and proved extremely successful.

Cosatto is consistently at the top of the leaderboard in 'Best Places to Work' and Glassdoor reviews are glowing. The team is effective, and the business is resilient and profitable. It's a triumph of values through adversity.

TIMPSON

With everything in life, there is a right way and a wrong way to do it. I love it when people are maverick and flourish. Most entrepreneurs I know have consistently done it the 'wrong way' and bounded forward through life.

Despite being over 150 years old, Timpson is thoroughly entrepreneurial. And as entrepreneurs, one 'best practice' mould they have completely smashed is for their values. Ideally, a values set contains seven items, max. Theirs has 28. Values 'should' be phrased consistently, in a logical order, and follow a theme. Theirs veer all over the place. There's no grammatical consistency at all.

How can ANYONE remember and work towards 28 apparently random items? And yet ... and yet. Over 5,000 Timpson people are completely committed to the Magic Dust. It's sprinkled everywhere, by everyone. Across the whole team there is dedication to delivering on its promises and meeting its high expectations.

It's because, from the Timpson family and throughout the team, there is a total commitment to those values. They are applied with a relentless vigour, stitched into every action and decision. The belief in those values is so strong that the business makes absolutely sure they deliver the goods. As with all real values, expectations are high - look at the values set and you'll see some tough stuff built in. As I say on repeat, values don't have to be 'nice' - they are about setting the bar high to help people achieve great things.

They call this
28-strong values
set their
Magic Dust.

1. **Aim to be the best**
2. **Enjoy change**
3. **Visit the business**
4. **Keep looking for ideas**
5. **Show leadership**
6. **Win hearts and minds**
7. **Weekly newsletter**
8. **No secrets**
9. **Upside down management**
10. **Amaze our customers**
11. **Obsessed with our people**
12. **Pick great people**
13. **No big shots**
14. **No head office**
15. **No politics**
16. **No cheats, no drongos**
17. **Great place to work**
18. **The bonus scheme**
19. **Training**
20. **Be fair**
21. **Know your people**
22. **Lifelong employment**
23. **Support people in trouble**
24. **Praise**
25. **Charity**
26. **Celebrate sucess**
27. **Have fun**
28. **Family business**

As John Timpson says:

> **"It took me ten years to ingrain this way of working into our culture. My deepest thinking colleagues realise that this is a never ending project ... We always live on a tightrope – it wouldn't take long for the magic dust to disappear."**

And in return the rewards are superb. Team members are treated with respect, kindness and generosity. Speak to someone at your local Timpson and see what they think: I can almost guarantee their eyes will light up as they talk about the business and their experiences in it.

Timpson calls their methodology 'upside down management'. The customer-facing staff on the floor in the shops are supported rather than controlled by management, and expected to use initiative.

It's genius. That positivity flows outwards to Timpson's customers and communities, helping the business to survive and thrive in changing marketplaces and through unexpected situations that have floored most of their competitors.

SINGAPORE

Imagine if you could take a whole country and treat it like a business - including vision and values? That's exactly what Lee Kuan Yew, also known as LKY, did when he took on the role of Singapore's Prime Minister in 1959 - the legacy of which is still growing and visible today, over sixty years later.

As founder of the People's Action Party, LSE and Cambridge-educated LKY lead the transformation of this 278m² island from a Colonial fishing village into multi-racial economic powerhouse. Singapore grew into the most advanced economy in South-East Asia, within twenty years having the second highest GDP per capita in the world.

Now a densely populated City Island State, it has for the last decade been the most expensive city in the world in which to live. That's balanced by its prominence in the key social indicators of education, healthcare, quality of life, personal safety and housing, with home-ownership at 91%.

Yet many people are critical of LKY, seeing his methods as draconian. His approach is collectivist, with firm rules vigorously enforced. 'No gum' has become the trope for Singaporean discipline, a global habit that often catches out visitors. But the imposition of values goes far further than that, with an attitude to reinforcement that to many people would seem extreme.

And that is why LKY is in this book. Because he set out with clearly articulated values, and pursued them scrupulously in every aspect of Singapore's behaviours to ensure successful delivery of his vision. They are even built into the independent state's flag. Those values are:

1. **Democracy**
2. **Peace**
3. **Progress**
4. **Justice**
5. **Equality**

On the flag, the crescent moon in the upper red band represents a new nation, the five stars contained by its arc each of the values.

LKY's attitude to the reinforcement of these values was uncompromising: "It is easy to start off with high moral standards, strong convictions, and determination to bead down corruption. But it is difficult to live up to these good intentions unless the leaders are strong and determined enough to deal with all transgressors, and without exceptions.".

Those actions included a ban on strikes, press censorship, taking opponents to court, corporal punishment for some convictions, limits on public protest, and tightly regulated daily life for Singapore's people. LKW would brook no contravention of the organisational culture he wanted to create.

So far, so rigid - an approach at odds with the established western sensibility of individualism and flexibility.

But in some ways LKW's system was a step ahead of us at the time: he believed that Singapore's 'multilingual, multicultural, multi-religious society' was the key to global success. He was clear in his view that homosexuality is genetic. Politically he enforced transparency and considered it important to publicly acknowledge mistakes.

The impacts of his approach included the high-speed realisation of his ambitious economic and social vision. High unemployment caused by the move from an established way of life was quickly dealt with, first through manufacturing and then inward investment. And the prevailing reputation of etiquette and ambition created a safe environment, and a strong message in the world of Singapore's attitude and capabilities.

You might not like Lee Kuan Yew, and you can support that view with plenty of evidence. But whatever your view of his approach it's undeniably a clear demonstration of the success that can be generated by rigorously applying Active Ethos.

SECTION TWO

ALL
ABOUT
YOU

Chapter 5
Getting to know you

Why are we stepping away from corporate culture into your personal values? Isn't that a bit of a diversion?

Yes and no.

Clearly our overriding aim is to get to grips with your business values. However, there is a lot to be said for alignment between your personal values and those of the place you work. That applies whether you lead it or not.

When people's values reflect those of the company they work for - and thus, also those of their colleagues - it creates an atmosphere of understanding. It means that people are generally making choices for good reasons, and that sense of shared understanding and purpose helps everyone to build good relationships.

There is another aspect to this, however.

It's very easy for us all to act as our job title, as a corporate animal. When we approach things that way, we tend to second guess situations. For this process to work, people need to have their hearts in it. Its success is based on people's emotional investment, not just actions.

The results are demonstrably better when I approach a corporate values project with people who are fully themselves. This exercise helps that to happen.

Overleaf you will see one hundred words. These are some of the most commonly reoccurring words in personal and corporate values.

Spend a bit of time reading through them, and jot down the ones that resonate with you. You're looking for the ones that really ping - to help, you might want to cross out the words that are completely different from you. That will give you a long list of relevant words, from which the heroes will stand out.

There may be words not included in here that are really important to you - that's absolutely fine, just note them down so you have them to hand as this exercise develops.

If you find this tricky, you might benefit from a full personal core values workshop, which you can read about on the Larkenby website.

1	Accountable	26	Diversity
2	Achieve	27	Duty
3	Aesthetic	28	Elegant
4	Affordable	29	Empathy
5	Ambition	30	Empowerment
6	Authentic	31	Equality
7	Belonging	32	Establishment
8	Bold	33	Ethics
9	Care	34	Excellence
10	Challenging	35	Extraordinary
11	Change	36	Fairness
12	Collaboration	37	Faith
13	Commitment	38	Family
14	Communication	39	First
15	Community	40	Flexibility
16	Competitive	41	Focus
17	Courage	42	Freedom
18	Craft	43	Fun
19	Creativity	44	Future
20	Decisive	45	Global
21	Deliberate	46	Growth
22	Delight	47	Hard work
23	Different	48	Health
24	Diligent	49	Heritage
25	Discipline	50	Honesty

51	Hope	76	Pride
52	Human	77	Professionalism
53	Humility	78	Profit
54	Humour	79	Quality
55	Imagination	80	Reliable
56	Impact	81	Repeatable
57	Improvement	82	Respect
58	Inclusion	83	Responsibility
59	Innovation	84	Results
60	Integrity	85	Safe
61	Justice	86	Selfless
62	Kind	87	Service
63	Leadership	88	Simplicity
64	Learning	89	Society
65	Loyalty	90	Speed
66	Memorable	91	Success
67	Opportunity	92	Sustainability
68	Optimistic	93	Teamwork
69	Ownership	94	Transparency
70	Passion	95	Trustworthy
71	People	96	Truth
72	Perserverence	97	Unorthodox
73	Philosophical	98	Wild
74	Polite	99	Witty
75	Practical	100	Youthful

For the next part of this exercise you might want to rope in a helper. Failing that, you can work on it yourself - maybe in front of a mirror, to give you a sense of two-way conversation.

Taking the very top words, probably about three, you are going to do two things.

Firstly, you are going to describe in the most evocative language possible how this value feels. Think of a real situation in which you have used it.

Where were you, who were you with, what was happening? Really dig into your senses to bring this story to life.

As you speak or write you should start to get a sense of it as if you were in the situation. Does it feel authentic? Does it feel like yours or someone else's?

You can jot this down in the space or talk it through with yourself or someone else.

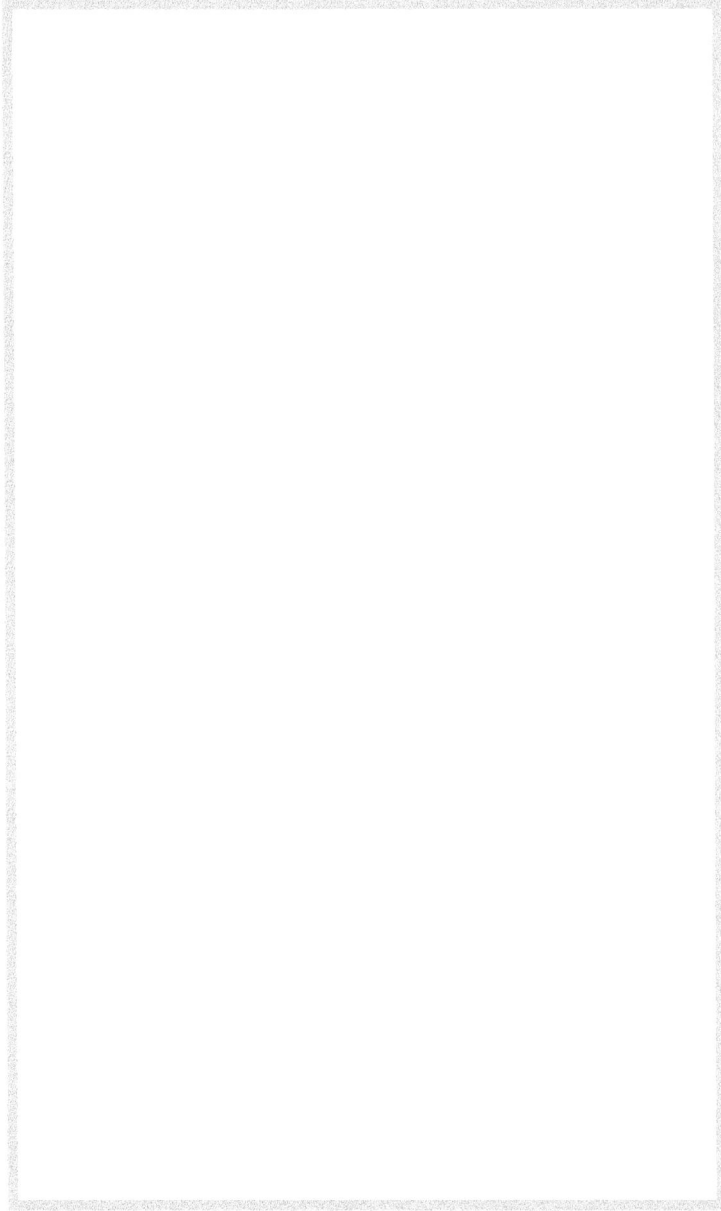

Now we are going to test it in another way, by pushing back on it or into it.

This will take a bit of imagination but it's worth it. What we are setting out to do is push really hard against your stated values to see if they stand up to pressure, or whether they crumble.

Here are two examples, to give you an idea of what we are aiming for. They are both business related but could equally well dip into family, sport, hobbies, travel - anything that is pertinent to your life.

The starting point for this is the phrase:

If this is your value, consider...

Let's say you picked out the word 'honesty', a laudable value if ever there was one. Generally people who are honest are trustworthy and decent. So let's push into it with this situation.

You mentor a junior colleague. Yesterday they came to you, visibly upset, having made the same mistake not just once but twice. They recognise their error, have spotted why it happened twice and know now how to prevent it in future. Pulling the strings you can pull in the business, you've helped to sort it out and no bones broken. However, the colleague's direct line manager – who can be a bit sharp – has caught wind of something and asks you what happened. Honesty being a stated value dictates you have to tell the line manager. This will likely land your mentee with a formal warning.

What would you do?

Now let's look at 'transparency'. This simple question might change your mind.

Because our values need to come to life across every aspect of our lives and our business, are you willing to be completely open about everyone's salaries? Including your own? Including your dividend and perks?

If not, you might want to reconsider that value.

It's also worth considering the difference between an embedded value and a shorter-term choice. There are some attitudes we take on to help us through an existing situation, which we can put to one side once that is resolved.

Values themselves sit deep, and are trustworthy enough for us to make tough decisions using them, decisions which might not always seem to be in our own best interests.

Professor Bill George, of Harvard, says:

"You do not know your true values until they are tested under pressure. Those who develop a clear sense of their values before they get into crisis are better prepared to keep their bearings and navigate through difficult decisions and dilemmas when the pressure mounts."

See what you can come up with (again, you can note your thoughts here). Consider situations that would challenge your value, or things you would absolutely have to do to honour it. Would you be willing to do so?

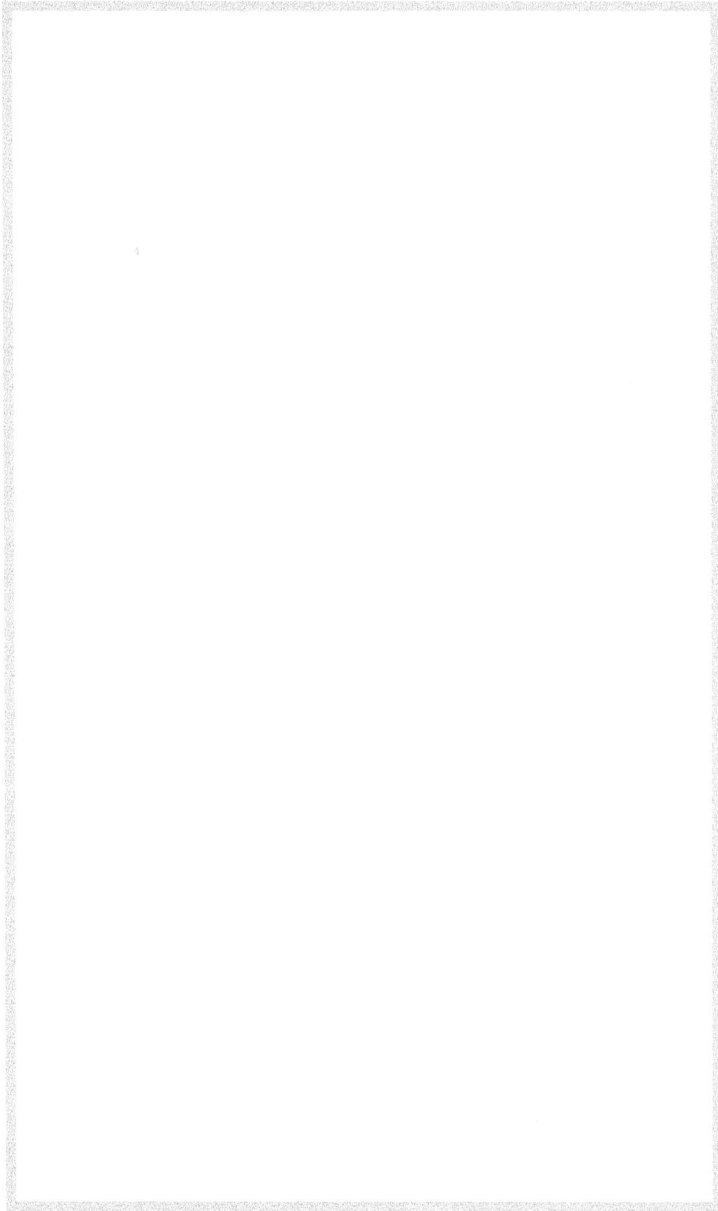

Finally, look back at that list of 100 values. Do you want to change your mind about any of them? For your records, jot down your list of top single word values here - allow somewhere between three and eight.

SECTION THREE

STEPS TO SUCCESS

Chapter 6
Six Steps to shape corporate values

This section is about how you'd go about drawing up your values set. Let's say your organisation had no formal values, or has realised the ones you have don't meet your needs.

You have the luxury of starting with a clean sheet, and if you take these steps you'll end up with a values set that will support Active Ethos.

1. AGREE WHY YOU ARE DOING THIS.

In the diagram, we can see how a vision is necessary to inspire everyone to live by the values. So your starting point is to develop that vision. In real life, it often grows alongside the values set - at least, its language does. You need to have a clear idea of the overriding ambition at the very start, even if it's unappetisingly phrased for now.

Consider also what you are looking to promote, and what you want to prevent. In other words, what's happening now that's great and you want more of, and what do you want to stamp out?

Bearing in mind that the journey from now to a fantastic culture is a hard one, think long and hard about why you are starting it. What is wrong that addressing your culture will address? What do you hope to achieve? Is it worth the effort?

This agreement needs to be at board level, with even the more reluctant members expressing their understanding of the need for this exercise and willingness to take part when needed.

VISION	➕	VALUES		
DRIVES		DRIVE	🟰	**ACTIVE ETHOS**
⬇		⬇		DRIVES
PEOPLE ➡		BEHAVIOUR		⬇
				CULTURE
				DELIVERS
				⬇
				VISION

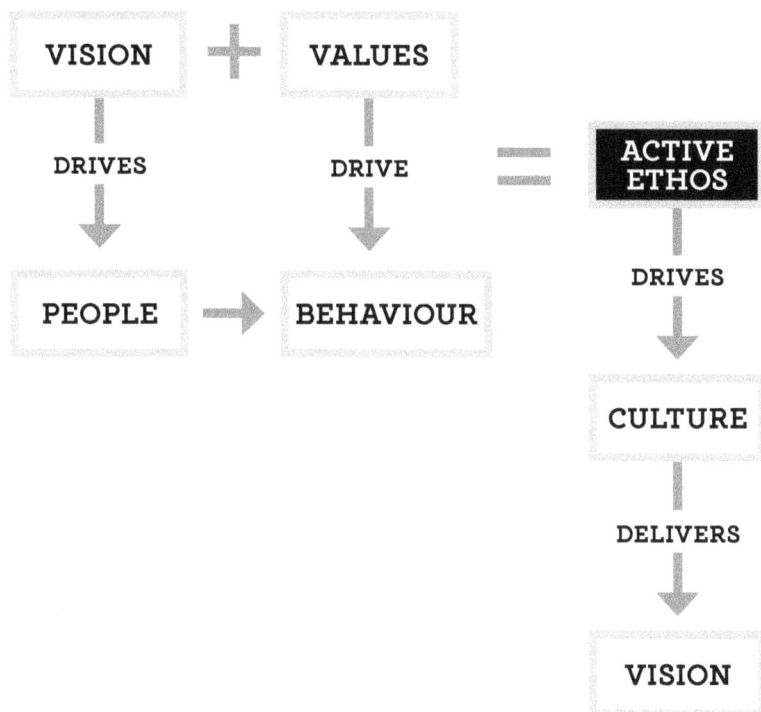

Vision drives people to behave in a way that is driven by values. It is that constant process of motivation and values-driven actions that we call Active Ethos. It in turn drives culture, which delivers the vision.

2. CHOOSE YOUR PEOPLE WISELY

Great values are created collaboratively, for all sorts of reasons - buy in and authenticity the two most obvious. So, having gained the commitment of your senior players, ask them to draw up a list of people from inside the organisation and outside, at all levels and with a range of remits.

You are looking at creating a sizable contact list of team members, customers, suppliers, community members and other stakeholders.

These people will be asked to share their stories about their connection to the business, being open about their views, experiences and expectations.

As a rule of thumb we recommend the final list has at least 25 names on it if you are a small business, and scale up from there as appropriate to your organisation. Clarity usually starts to form after around 15-20 conversations, so you don't need hundreds of people.

Consider who will be living by the values. Who will benefit from the changes they bring to the business. Think ahead, also, to when you have agreed the values set, and started to roll them out to become your culture - you'll be looking for a team of Culture Champions.

This is a good starting point for creating that group, so on that list of people you want to include some of the stars, who you trust and want to honour with the responsibility of helping you bring this to life.

Have one person gather all details into one list, which ensures duplicates can be eradicated; then invitations need to go out with an explanation of why you want to speak to them. Not all those you contact will respond, and you may need to ask round for more suggestions.

Of politeness, this needs to happen a few weeks before you intend to have the conversations, so people have plenty of warning.

3. DIG DOWN FOR GREAT STORIES

Having put together this list and had sufficient responses to get the information you need, it's time for the conversations. The aim of these is for the people you interview to get as relaxed and chatty as possible.

To encourage them to open up you might want to ask someone from outside the business to have the chats - it has many additional benefits, as often those conversations reveal things that need fixing which might otherwise have stayed buried until it was too late to sort out.

Record them the best way for you - you can sound record them, even on your phone; if you're a jotter then write your notes. It's polite (and legally required) to let the interviewees know what you are doing, and what their stories will be used for.

When I have these conversations I start with a short list of questions, which I will send to the interviewees in advance. This allows them to prepare and ensures we start with clarity. However, the goal is to move off piste as soon as possible, so people fall into their natural way of speaking and open up to a more honest conversation.

Our goal is to find some personal stories, which reveal their perception of your company in its current form. You will observe not just their content but also the language people use, phrases and words that reoccur, the mood and character of the stories. Over the course of these conversations, patterns and rhythms start to appear. These have enormous value to you in preparing the values set.

It's a positive process. You are digging into 'us at our best'. Be open to negatives too - they have value, and allow you to address them as well as recognising what your new values can be used to eradicate - but really focus on drawing out the great things.

It's a process that has a rhythm of its own. Some conversations will flow, some will stutter. Some people will find it hard to state positives and others will gush with approval. Some will arrive with a message they really want to get across. After a few the sheer amount of information will feel overwhelming.

Don't worry! I liken it to a snowglobe, which you shake repeatedly. Soon, the flakes will settle and you will see a clear picture. It happens every time. You will start to see the things that bind people's view of the business, that drive their ambition, that they are impressed by or wish existed. You will recognise phrases and words, you'll get an insight to character and personality.

4. CRAFT VALUES THAT ZING AND FLY

Having had the conversations and made sense of what they revealed, you're ready to draw up a draft values set. Here are some tips for ways to make them compelling and effective.

1. Filter through the service or product you offer
2. Make them creatively bold (this is exciting)
3. ... or matter of fact (this is easy to access)
4. Use them to set expectations, not to support an easy ride
5. Make them clear, memorable, decisive and actionable
6. Express it in the language your people (not business people) use
7. Ensure they apply to everyone, everywhere
8. Keep them real and slightly daunting
9. .... and keep them brief, and few (so they are memorable).

Having drawn up these draft values, you want to take them back out to some of the interviewees to gauge their reactions, and make any changes that those reactions lead to. They'll also need to be reviewed by your core senior team and any other groups whose buy-in is necessary and will be impacted by involvement.

Don't lose sight of the purpose, however, or what the conversations taught you - these are your values, not an exercise in compromise. Make changes which will improve them and support their success.

And now, you have a values set, ready to launch and nurture!

5. GIVE EVERYONE A REASON TO CARE

This is where we come back to the vision. Whilst you agreed corporate ambitions in business terms at the start of this process, the conversations have unlocked its character and language. You'll have a clearer idea of people's definition of success and reward.

Now's the time to collate that and use it to create a vision that gives everyone something to aim for.

What is their north star, their world cup, their gold, their honey?

Tie up your commercial goals into an evocative exciting image, expressed in the language of your people, that gives everyone a reason to care.

6. PUT THE ACTIVE IN ACTIVE ETHOS.

It's very simple. Launch the values and vision with clear explanations of what they mean, and actions to stitch them into the daily life of the business. Nominate Culture Champions to support that happening and help you keep up the momentum. Build in actions and expressions everywhere and through everyone. Review progress, and experiment with new things as you go. And then:

REPEAT REPEAT REPEAT REPEAT REPEAT
REPEAT REPEAT REPEAT REPEAT REPEAT
REPEAT REPEAT REPEAT REPEAT REPEAT
REPEAT REPEAT REPEAT REPEAT REPEAT
REPEAT REPEAT REPEAT REPEAT REPEAT
REPEAT REPEAT REPEAT REPEAT REPEAT
REPEAT REPEAT REPEAT REPEAT REPEAT
REPEAT REPEAT REPEAT REPEAT REPEAT
REPEAT REPEAT REPEAT REPEAT REPEAT

As Jeff Bezos says:

"Our culture is friendly and intense, but if push comes to shove we'll settle for intense."

SECTION FOUR

FORMING YOUR PLAN

Chapter 7
Make your ethos active

Now, at this point you might expect to sharpen your pencil and settle down to come up with some thoughts on your own company values.

I'm sorry, but that's not going to happen.

Here's why. Creating a good set of values and using them as the platform to grow your culture can fall prey to a number of errors: and you sitting on your own or with your board colleagues to draw up the values would be number one. Get them on side, but have those conversations and ensure everyone feels involved.

Here are just some of the things that can go wrong when you start to work on your values, and as you bring them to life.

You haven't involved everyone from the off, so it feels like your project not theirs	Your values are not clearly phrased or explained, so no one is quite sure what to do with them
Your values do not align with your brand communications, which should in fact be an articulation of your culture	One level of the business isn't living it - if you, or the Saturday staff, or anyone in between is laissez-faire about them, they will fail
There's not enough trust or respect for people to buy into the need for this, or even follow the actions built around it	You're not using it when things are great (lost in the pace) or tough (which is when they should really be most helpful)
You're not using it to challenge, which is again one of their greatest benefits	You've got bored and moved onto a new project - this is a marathon, not a sprint. Actually, make that an ultra-marathon.

So let's create a plan that will help you get this working. What we need is to look across the whole organisation, its people and their areas of focus.

James Timpson describes 'breaking down bits of the business to see what we can do to increase it'. That is in a commercial context, but as a values-driven organisation it's clear that it also applies to their culture.

To take this approach, it helps to break things down into areas of focus. We describe this as the 'Five Ps', and they are:

1. **People**
2. **Publicity**
3. **Partners**
4. **Processes**
5. **Performance**

Over the next few pages you'll find some of the ways you can build actions around values in each of these areas to start to embed them into the organisation. These are a starting point, largely included to trigger your thinking. Jot down thoughts as they arise.

When considering actions, think of who can own them, and how you can evaluate them - this will allow you to build a team around this and create a clear sense of progress. Bear in mind that much of this, you will be doing already. It's often just a matter of building the values into your existing activities. It can be very simple and literal (detailed specifically in contracts) or sit under the surface (included in marketing briefs, for example, to ensure that the resulting campaign takes your values into account).

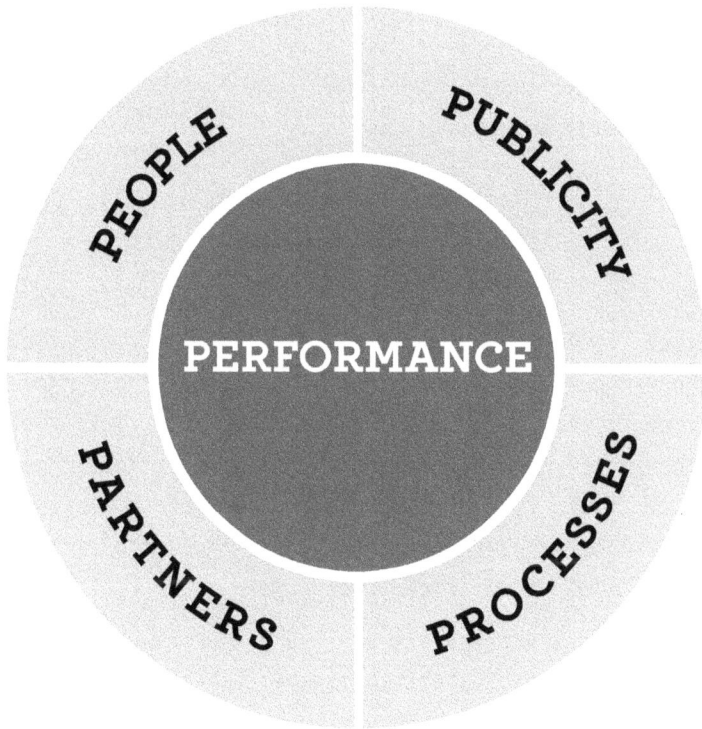

PEOPLE

PUBLICITY

PERFORMANCE

PARTNERS

PROCESSES

PEOPLE

Start with yourself. If you are the person whose decision it was to make this happen, you're going to need to commit to it. It should feel personal. When I led the programme at my business, it became my number one priority.

Other people came in around me to lead elements of it, but had I dropped my interest it would have signalled to them that they could allow their focus to waver too. I built actions into my daily to-do list, and had recurring activities that I diarised at the start of the year - team one to one coaching, ethos awards, and team updates, for example.

Others' journeys through employment can be built around your values. Include them in job ads, introduce them to your interviews planning and trial days, if you offer those. Invite people to tell you their stories that reflect your values - never just ask if they share them. How do they see your values come to life in the business, from an outside perspective? (You never know what you might learn.)

Once you have hired, put values at the heart of the induction process, and as that morphs into ongoing personal development do the same. Include the values in employment contracts, terms and conditions, welcome packs and job descriptions.

I've spoken of the benefits of career development sessions with team members - even if it means that their pace of development can challenge your own role! - and the values are a crucial part of this. Assuming your values are designed to build capabilities towards a bold vision, they can become very useful stepping stones in Personal Development Plans. Similarly they can be built into training plans.

Use them as the criteria in 360 reviews, and invite people to mark themselves against the values as well as each other. I kept this very simple, asking them to grade themselves 'always, sometimes, not enough' and give a brief explanation of why they came to that answer. Once-off this is useful, but tracked over time it's fascinating.

If you have team members who are stars but whose specific role has limited advancement opportunities at the moment, the role of Culture Champion (or whatever terminology fits your business) presents a fantastic chance to lead improvement, meet senior people on a regular basis, and demonstrate their capabilities in a wider arena. You'll want people from every level of the organisation, and from across all departments.

For people with ambition (even if it's latent) this is an extraordinary opportunity to vault the layers of the organisation straight up to direct board access. You might consider building rewards for them in the shape of a senior mentor.

At the start you'll brief them on their role - what actions are going to be put into place, how they can support take-up, which teams they are focusing on, what metrics there are for success - but as time goes by, the goal is to see them start to take ownership. Monthly/bi-monthtly meetings, perhaps over lunch with the company CEO, allow them to share their experiences, consider what's working and what's not, and agree on adjustments. Other rewards can also be used to develop your Active Ethos. Bonuses, in whatever shape you award them, can be directly linked to delivery on the values. (If your mind immediately leaps to bonuses being awarded based on annual profit, then maybe profit needs to sit within one of your values.) On a more light hearted level, all-team get togethers with Values Awards give those gatherings purpose, encourage them to happen and publicly celebrate the success of embodying your corporate culture.

As a direct result of these activities, and others you devise, you will see a marked improvement in people's commitment to their work, their colleagues and the company. And the outcome of that is improved performance.

When people leave (and incidentally, as you work through this programme, you will lose people who feel at odds with the culture you are creating), approaching this with your values front and centre will take your reputation forward. Whatever the reason for people's departure, ensure that their final weeks are lived according to your ethos, by them, you, and everyone around them.

PUBLICITY

In many ways, brand was the starting point of my own values journey. During my career in branding agencies I grew to feel very strongly that brand is nothing more or less than an articulation of culture. Just as with culture, brand is inferred from behaviour: dictated by the recipient not the giver. In that respect, you could say that brand IS culture.

I recognise that this is a challenging perspective for many people, and so I can pull it back to the suggestion that your values become the strategic pillars for your brand, just as they are the behaviour-drivers for your culture. If that looks impossible, then you may need to reconsider your values or your brand strategy. Once you have these in place, you can build your brand's style - its design, language and channels - around those values so that it represents your organisation in a deep-set authentic way.

Brand is big-picture stuff, but often when it comes to injecting values across the business you want to go very granular. Let's be literal about this. You'll often hear people cite that having your values on display in reception or on mugs isn't enough for them to become culture. That's 100% true, but it still needs to be done!

So think about where you can get the values printed, sign-written, programmed or stuck. As I say in workshops: if it doesn't run away fast enough, get the values on it. Doors, windows, loo cubicles. Vans, uniforms, signage. Information screens, welcome boards, wayfinding. Screensavers, mugs, pens. The list goes on. What can you think of?

Looking at external communications, you'll want to build your values into marketing briefs. This ensures that they are taken into account when your agency or internal team comes up with campaign ideas, develops your digital communications tools, plans media and SEO. It's unlikely in most cases that the values will be included in their full form: but their inclusion in briefs ensures any work fully reflects their content, tone and purpose.

However, on your website, social media biogs, press release boilerplates and materials for presentations, events and exhibitions, you may well want to include them item by item. Introduce them with an explanation of how they combine to deliver clarity and guarantee outcomes. It's an incredibly powerful promise.

Whilst this might sound tasteless, any charity, community or other CSR activities you undertake fit into this section. You most likely do them out of altruism, but that doesn't mean they should not reflect and do not promote your values. They are, after all, a touchpoint for audiences to your business. So when you choose charity partners, community actions, even the style of support - whether that's simply financial input or ongoing direct involvement by your team - consider what you are looking to reflect in your culture.

PARTNERS

Whether your partnerships are formal or informal, and irrespective of who issued the invitation to partnership, hard-wiring your values into them helps them to deliver on your culture. It means everyone knows where you stand from the off and helps to create strong bonds of understanding.

Let's look at your supplier relationships. When you are first inviting companies to tender for your business, even if that's just by way of a quotation, it's a good opportunity to acquaint them with your values. In having a quote accepted they become part of your ecosystem, and that means that they can expect you to live up to your values, and you can expect them to do the same in their dealings with you and mutual clients.

Just as with recruitment, build your values into the initial communications. That might be bid invitations through your procurement teams, a briefing document issued direct from the person who needs it, or in a phone call or email. Ensure that bidder responses demonstrate an understanding of your values, and show how they will be reflected in the supplier's work with you. If your selection process involves interviews, meetings and test projects, build opportunities to demonstrate understanding of the values into them.

Once you have selected your preferred partner, build the values into the signed-for documentation. Whether that's a relatively informal 'code of behaviour' or Service Level Agreement (SLA), or a full-blown legal contract, the values and some explanation of how and why they are embedded into behaviours is completely relevant. As we all know, it's impossible to get a true picture of partner organisations until we actually start to work together, so having signatures from vendor and buyer gives clarity to any necessary conversations that crop up around expectations as the partnership rolls out.

This applies in the other direction too. One of the most powerful moments I had at the beginning of my company's Active Ethos journey was pitching to a lapsed client. The relationship had petered out slightly uncomfortably a few years previously. When we met, our Ethos was the second slide in our deck. "This is our Ethos," I said. "We hold ourselves to it. You can, too." The company's Chief Executive was in the meeting, and as I showed them and explained it, I observed a clear change in his body language, from arms-crossed "I'm here because I said I'd be" to leaning-forward interest. We won the project. Clearly that was because of our work, not just our values: but they built a level of trust that definitely oiled the wheels.

So build your values into your responses to briefs, literally and stylistically. People intuit the authenticity of your stated values from all sorts of cues: use of language, visual style, level of detail, even the layout of hard data. All these come across even without you in the room. Focus on giving them the best chance of survival amongst your peers with a self-selected target audience. Having won the project, and with clients you already have, build your values into SLAs, contracts, Terms and Conditions, and any other documentation. It goes without saying that the place in which your values most come to life are in project delivery.

A note here - it is entirely reasonable to ask your clients to live up to your values, just as you ask your suppliers and other business partners. It's completely up to you to decide how far to push this. Patagonia, for example, has refused to stitch corporate logos onto its gilets for any businesses that don't protect the environment, thus chopping off most of their lucrative work from big city businesses. This change came straight from the team responsible for the embroidering, not Patagonia's board: as ever, they are an exemplar of living their ethos.

Even for informal or non-corporate relationships like exploratory collaborations, external coaching, charity partnerships and so on, it's worth building some formality couched in the 'policy' context. This clarity helps ensure that consistency of values is maintained, even in the greyer areas of your working lives.

PROCESSES

Not only will your values come to life through your processes, but they might also define which methodologies you choose to introduce. For example, if a value covered simplicity you would look to embrace simple documentation like one page business plans, quotes and proposals; whereas if a value was about attention to detail you'd want to use something that gets a lot more granular.

There is a huge range of strategy models available, and in considering which one to put in place to help you maintain corporate direction and overview, look at them alongside your values to help you choose the one that works best for you. I ran my old business on Reclaro's 1-3-5 system, which suited our scale and energy; a client with a logistics business swears by Traction/EOS. A manufacturer with exemplar values builds all team motivation around the 3R's system and has seen great success.

There is also a host of management methods from which you can select whole systems or pieces. One social housing company's unwieldy customer service structure was completely transformed through reference to the time honoured 'Toyota Way'.

So do your homework and, as with all important decisions, lean on your values for advice.

In talking about partnerships, I mentioned that you can use your values in the sales process as a guarantee of outcomes. Since you are using them as the means to encourage everyone to be their best everyday it is reasonable to build them into your project planning as metrics or points on the way. This embeds them in a practical way which helps to ensure they are maintained by the team, and observed in action by your client.

The number one thing is to ensure that whatever formality you bring in, the values are deployed to ensure consistency in the day-to-day, repetitive tasks - that's where they are most open to scrutiny, where they can deliver the most efficiency and impact, and where, without sustained attention, they are most likely to be neglected. Keep it up!

PERFORMANCE

The fifth p, performance, is also the end result of all the others. It's the thing that delivers success, and it's the outcome of a fantastic values-driven culture.

Here are just some places you'll find Active Ethos delivering exceptional performance.

TEAM

- Development
- Recruitment
- Retention
- Morale
- Loyalty
- Responsibility

BRAND

- Desirability
- Standout
- Value
- Authenticity
- Reputation

QUALITY CONTROL

- Personal accountability
- Peer accountability
- Standard setting
- Pride

PERFORMANCE

- Efficiency
- Profitability
- Striving
- Growth

SALES

- Clarity
- Messaging
- Guarantee expectations
- Visibility
- Contracts

INDUSTRY PEERS

- Exemplar status
- Recognition
- Talent magnet
- M&A benefits

SUMMARY

I hope you have enjoyed this book, and found useful stories and activities in it that will help you to harness your values to create a high-performance culture. In closing, this is my promise to you.

It will not be easy. Your focus on it will not be understood by those around you in the early days. But once you are on the right path, bringing people around you, heading towards something exciting together: you will, very quickly, start to see an extraordinary transformation.

And remember:

1. Stick with it: this is a long haul

2. Say no: to potential team, clients (old and new), diverse temptations

3. Be Active Ethos's constant, unrelenting, faithful champion

4. Be prepared to change the things you thought were set in stone

5. Put it everywhere, on everything, via everyone, incessantly

6. Your vision will change. Your team will change. Your activities might change. **Your values will stand firm throughout.**

ABOUT ERIKA CLEGG

Erika Clegg is a corporate values consultant, writer and startup advisor. She hosts the values podcast REV, and founded Larkenby, a corporate values consultancy, in 2019. As a passionate advocate for the subject, she is an award-winning speaker for organisations including international CEO coaching group Vistage, and works with clients including the Prison Reform Trust.

From 2006-2022, Erika owned Spring, a multi-award-winning brand communications agency with a strong community support ethos. Erika has been a director of the Design Business Association and New Anglia LEP; Route Panel Advisor for the Institute of Apprentices; trustee of various cultural and community charities, and Ambassador for The Right Course. She is a Fellow of the Royal Society for the Encouragement of Arts, Manufactures and Commerce and holds a Non Executive Director qualification from Cranfield.

Erika is a Deputy Lieutenant of Suffolk and lives in Southwold with her family, pets and a Peloton habit.

www.ingramcontent.com/pod-product-compliance
Lightning Source LLC
Chambersburg PA
CBHW042122190326
41519CB00031B/7580